D0408214

Mandala

sacred symbols

Mandala

Thames and Hudson

THE CIRCLE
AND THE CENTRE

although most immediately associated with the religions and cults of India and Tibet, the mandala, literally 'circle', is one of the most potent symbols of humankind. Its circular form and concentric structure reflect the shape of the universe outside and the sense of perfection within. Concentration on its form and content is an aid to prayer and meditation, leading eventually to a complete at-oneness with the world.

This cosmic mandala fresco in the Temple Court of the Paro Dzong fortress, West Bhutan, incorporates the 'mystic spiral', representation of the primary movement of the universe.

Frontispiece An eighteenth-century Tibetan hanging painting of the Supreme Buddha Vajrasattva, synthesizing mandalas.

the cosmic mandala

representation of the universe as a series
of concentric rings has been common in many cultures,
consistently reappearing in art and ritual. In this
context, the mandala can be seen as an evocation of the
universe, of galaxies swirling around a centre, of planets
revolving around the sun. At the same time, it is a
model of the soul's journey from the periphery to the
centre of all understanding. This is a journey common
to the initiates of Tantric cults, the aborigines of
Australasia and even psychiatric patients in search
of wholeness in a fragmented world.

Representations of
the universe and its orbits,
surrounded by outer space,
may be used as meditational
aids, their circular form
suggesting a simple mandala-
yantra (a seventeenth-century
example from Gujarat).

the island continent

althougb the cosmograms of Tantric belief were certainly a way of codifying external phenomena, of organizing current knowledge of the universe, their mandala-like form lent them a complexity of functions. They are focused on a single point, the mythical Mount Meru, around which is the earth, Jambu-dirīpa, with concentric circles representing cosmic fields, spheres, and atmospheric zones within the sphere which separates the visible from the non-visible world. In Tantric belief the central point of Mount Meru may also be identified with the centre point of the human body — thus man becomes at one with the universe, which radiates as a flat circle from his spinal tube, the Merudanda *or* Sushumnā.

Opposite Meditation on formal representations of the universe is designed to achieve identification with the fundamental forces of the cosmos. Cosmographical diagrams, such as this eighteenth-century painted-cloth example from Rajasthan, show *Jambu-dirīpa*, the island continent, surrounded by energy fields and atmospheric zones.

movement and rest

the image of the cosmos as a still point around which
turn various degrees of creation is applicable in
many contexts. It may be made immensely complex by
having the centre occupied by a potent religious image:
the Buddha, perhaps, or a temple, with other saints and
icons at the cardinal points. In its simplest yet
most intense form the centre of the Hindu and Buddhist
mandala is the deratā, the ultimate divine principle,
uniting object and subject as they spin out from
the centre, which may be cosmic,
but which may equally be that of the
human body.

Opposite This seventeenth-century gouache mandala
from Rajasthan is a simple yet potent symbol of the cosmos
in simultaneous evolution and dissolution, in tension and repose.
In yoga, this symbol is the powerful enneagram, whose exact
meaning must remain a secret but which is universally known to
invoke simultaneously perpetual motion and perpetual rest.

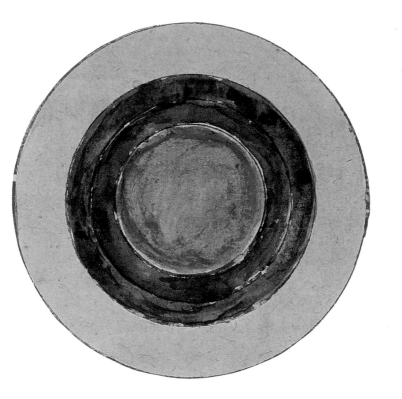

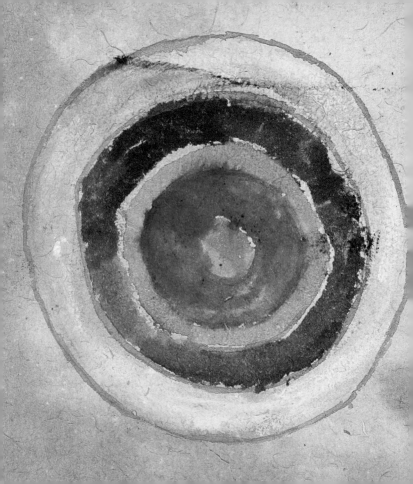

a map of the cosmos

So the mandala is no longer a cosmogram but a psychocosmogram, the scheme of the disintegration from the One to the Many and of reintegration from the Many to the One, to that Absolute Consciousness, entire and luminous...

(Giuseppe Tucci)

Opposite The essential, universal pattern of the mandala is beautifully expressed in this simple seventeenth-century gouache from Uttar Pradesh. Its representation of the limitless space of the cosmos also symbolizes all essential structures – the society which rotates around the throne of the king, the universe around its central mountain, our own bodies around their axial points.

t*he mandala is both a universal symbol and a symbol of the universe. But its use in the rituals and liturgies of various religions and cults and, indeed, in modern psychoanalysis is only a part of its whole significance; it is also the essential plan of the whole universe, balancing centrifugal and centripetal forces, combining beginning and end. It is the ultimate symbol of wholeness; its centre is unity, equidistant from every point of the outer curve of the circle. In grasping the whole significance of this symbol, the individual – whatever his or her culture – experiences the sense of liberation which comes from the realization of the unity of all phenomena and experience.*

a gateway to the divine

the potency of concentric circles around a centre point, the most intense expression of the divine, pervades all cultures and religions. Among the Huichol tribes of California and Mexico, such a vision of circles, the *nierika*, is a prayer offering, a reflection of the face of the god, and a means of realizing the most concentrated experience of the sacred, symbolized by the centre point.

This modern painting by Michael Brown (Rising Eagle) shows a celebrant and symbolic slain deer before a great *nierika*.

a chinese mirror

Certain early Chinese mirrors are effectively mandalas (opposite) – classic schemes of the universe: the circles of the heavens, the square of the earth and the central point of Unification. The first principle of the universe, the Tao, is identified with the centre which is usually referred to in an inscription: 'May your eight sons and nine grandsons govern the centre'. Nine is the perfect number, made up of four females, Yin, and five males, Yang, represented by the moon and the sun.

If you ascend the T'ai-shan mountain, you will see the holy men; they eat the essence of jade and drink the limpid spring; they have attained the Way of Heaven; all things are in their natural state; they yoke the Hornless Dragon to their chariot; they mount the floating clouds; may you have high office and rank, may you preserve your sons and grandsons.

(I-Ching)

a christian 'mandala'

*t*he circle as an image for concentrating
spiritual thought and feeling is omnipresent in
Christianity, especially in its more mystical
representations. It appears in the form of rose
windows, in labyrinths, and is one obvious way
of connecting the points of the cross, the basic
symbol of the Christian religion. The cross itself
is strongly associated with the idea of a cross-
roads at which essential energy is concentrated.
It is also the Tree of Life, with its inevitable
connotations of decay, death and rebirth.
Significantly the circle in this fourteenth-century
French miniature (opposite) is shown
quartered by a cross, while Angels turn the outer
wheel of the universe, indicating that it is driven
by the creative energy of God.

the hermetic universe

*t*he obliteration of distinctions, the experience of the essential unity of the cosmos, and therefore of God, are concepts shared by the mystics of all the world's great religions. Such experience has, perhaps, played a smaller part in the rituals and liturgies of the West, mainly because the Christian Church has always interposed itself between the individual and direct experience of the supreme enlightenment.

The endless circle is a symbol of the expanding universe – the cycle of repetition and renewal. In Robert Fludd's engraving of 1617 (*opposite*) the outer circles of the diagram are those of Supernatural Fire with cherubim and seraphim, symbols of divine energy. Nature is shown as a naked woman, chained by her right wrist to God (represented as 'JHVH', Jahveh) and by her left to the monkey, symbol of lower nature.

(*Utriusque Cosmi*)

Nevertheless, certain figures and groups within the Western tradition – notably those associated with Hermetic and Qabalistic beliefs and practices – have expressed the longing for the ultimate experience in diagrammatic mandala-like forms which incorporate archetypal symbols.

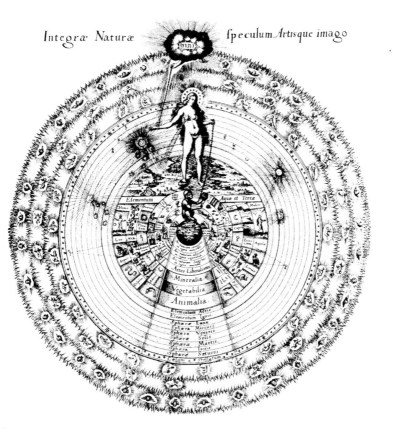

Integræ Naturæ ſpeculum, Artiſque imago

THE WAY TO THE GODS

the mandala is a compact mystical diagram, concentrating spiritual energy; it is an icon of religious experience and, at the same time, a visible manifestation of godhood. It is the dwelling place of the highest deity and often also of subsidiary divinities. In Buddhist mandalas the Supreme Buddha may be shown wearing a mantle and royal tiara, denoting his status as Universal Monarch. Among the Tantric cults, especially, the deity may be represented by a linear mandala, the yantra.

This is the truth: as from a fire aflame thousands of sparks come forth, even so from the Creator an infinity of beings have life and to him return again.

But the spirit of light above form, never-born, within all, outside all, is in radiance above life and mind, and beyond this creation's Creator.

From him comes all life and mind, and the senses of all life. From him comes space and light, air and fire and water, and this earth that holds us all.

(Mundaka Upanishad)

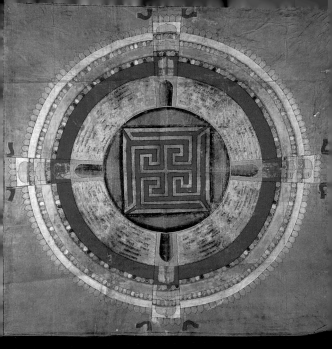

The centre of this diagram of the cosmos, from eighteenth-
century Rajasthan, takes the form of a maze-like swastika, a
graphic representation of the journey the initiate must make to
achieve a sense of at-oneness with the Supreme Being.

The outer triangles of this elaborate Śrī Yantra are peopled with divinities representing the sub-divided forces of the Great Goddess (Nepal, *c.* 1700).

śiva-śakti

the most important and most universal Hinduist mandala-yantra is the Śri Yantra, a complex arrangement of triangles and lotus leaves expressing the whole motive energy of the universe and the delicate balance of the male and female principles. The fine downward-pointing triangles symbolize Śakti, the female principle representative of all in the cosmos which is active and creative; the four upward-pointing ones symbolize Śiva, the male principle and supreme consciousness. How the triangles intersect is clearly open to interpretation, and the initiate may read them in a number of ways. However, the dualism is more apparent than real: what this yantra is expressing is the unity of the cosmic consciousness with which the individual can identify.

To the utterly at-one with Śiva

there's no dawn,
no new moon,
no noonday,
nor equinoxes,
nor sunsets,
nor full moons...

(*Devara Dasimayya*)

the god of the waters

those Hindu ceremonies and meditational rites to invoke a divine essence require a round receptacle to be placed in the centre of the mandala or yantra. This is filled with various substances and is the receptacle in which the deity will first lodge before passing into the supplicant. Varuna, to whom this mandala is devoted, is the deity of cosmic order and also 'Lord of Waters'.

Now I shall speak of the yantra of the Planets, which promotes all kinds of peace... When one has worshipped the planets... the eight Governors of the directions should be worshipped... (including) Varuna, god of the waters in the west, who is white, sits on a Makara monster, holding a noose.

(Śiva in the *Mahānurvana Tantra*)

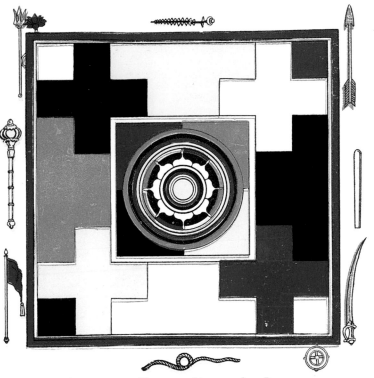

A contemporary Varuna mandala-yantra from Benares;
the outer enclosure is guarded by the emblems of the
deities and regents of space.

The Bodhisattvas, those figures of boundless compassion, have their own mandala-yantras which take on the imagery of the cosmic 'whole' and may therefore be used for meditation and illumination. These yantras invoke the goddess Tara, one of the female Bodhisattvas, whose name means 'She who causes one to cross', alluding to crossing over the turbulent river of existence to peace on the other side (Rajasthan, 18th century, gouache on paper).

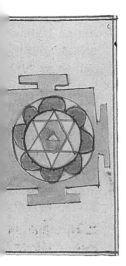

Few cross the river of time and are able to reach Nirvana. Most of them run up and down only on this side of the river.

But those who when they know the law follow the path of the law, they shall reach the other shore and go beyond the realm of death.

Leaving behind the path of darkness and following the path of light, let the wise man leave his home life and go into a life of freedom. In solitude that few enjoy, let him find his joy supreme: free from possessions, free from desires, and free from whatever may darken his mind.

(*The Dhammapada*)

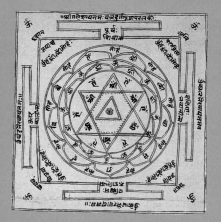

A power diagram of
Kālī for use in
meditation
(Nepal, *c.* 1761,
gouache on paper).

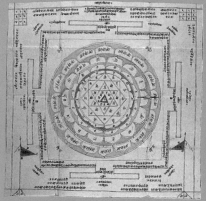

kālī

Said to have been born from the brow of the great goddess Durgā during a battle between the gods and demons, Kālī is one of the most fervently worshipped deities in the Tantric pantheon. She is often portrayed as being of terrifying aspect, garlanded with severed heads, brandishing a sword in one hand and holding a skull in the other. Yet, though such imagery suggests death and destruction, it also implies their opposite: creation and life. At the centre of the yantra, Kālī is the creative force of the world, the embodiment of the ceaseless cycles of destruction and renewal which transcend the everyday world of facile appearance. Through meditation with the aid of the Kālī mandala-yantra the neophyte will pierce through to a truer reality.

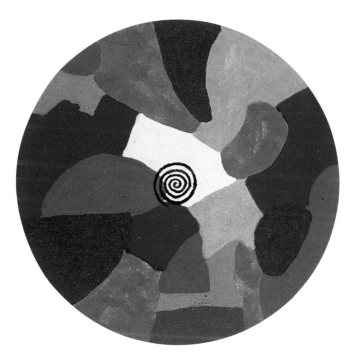

Yantra of the cosmic form of
Madhusudan, another name for Vishnu
(Rajasthan, *c.* 18th century, ink and colour
on paper).

vishnu

One of the great high gods of Hinduism, Vishnu appears in a number of incarnations, including Krishna, Rāma and the Buddha. He is the deity worshipped by one of the major sects of Tantrikas, the Vaishnavas – the others are Śaivas (devotees of Śiva) and Śāktas (those of Śakti – the female principle). Legend has it that the sacred places of Tantric worship were created on the sites where the parts of Śakti fell to the ground after she had been dismembered by Vishnu.

a goddess of abundance

An important monthly ritual of Nepalese Buddhism is the worship of the Bodhisattva Amoghapāśa-Lokeśvara, the goddess Vasundharā (Earth). Suitably placated, she is responsible for well-being and the prevention of poverty. In mandalas devoted to specific deities, the god resides in the centre, also known as the 'palace'. It has been suggested that this form was originally inspired by the Mesopotamian ziggurat, which was itself a cosmogram of the universe.

A sixteenth
century Nepales
painted mandal
to Vasundharā
goddess of th
earth and plenty

krishna

as the great love god of India, the figure of Krishna occupies a central role in vernacular Hindi literature and art. His couplings with cow-girls, known as Gopis, were legendary, and were frequently enshrined in mandala-like representations of the spring-time round dance, the ras-lila, in which the Gopis were sexually united with the all-powerful god, the earthly reflection of a cosmic union of male and female principles.

The round dance of spring, culminating in the union of the Gopis with Krishna (Jaipur, *c.* 1800, gouache on paper).

the buddhas

the correspondence between the macrocosm and the microcosm in the mandalas of Tantric Buddhism is often expressed in forceful, figurative terms. Like the Hindu vision of the universe, Buddhism saw both external phenomena and internal experience in quinary terms: five elements, five colours, five objects of the senses, the five senses themselves. The Buddhism of the Diamond Vehicle sees the supreme original consciousness, Vajrasattva, as divided into five Buddhas: Vairocana, 'The Brilliant One'; Absobhya, 'The Unshakable'; Ratnasambhava, 'The Matrix of the Jewel'; Amitabha, 'The Infinite Light', and Amoghasiddhi, 'The Infallible Realization'. Each one is associated with a particular colour, personality type and a passion or human shortcoming.

This eighteenth-century Tibetan *tanka* (*opposite*) shows the mandalas of the Peaceful Buddhas, the Knowledge-Holders and the Wrathful Buddhas, of the Buddhas who preside over the realms of reincarnation, and of the Guardian of the Four Directions.

mandalas of the dead

the mandala reproduced opposite
and the one which follows represent
deities of the other world and are thus
intended to both instruct the adept
in the ways of death and help him
prepare for his own. According to
The Tibetan Book of the Dead,
the newly deceased passes through
a preliminary period of consideration
during which he must face the 'lights
of the six places of rebirth', which will
eventually determine his fate. During
this period the dead is confronted first
by the benign Buddhas for seven days,
and then by the wrathful ones.

By what earthly
path could you
entice the
Buddha who,
enjoying all, can
wander through
the pathless ways
of the Infinite? –
the Buddha who
is awake, whose
victory cannot
be turned into
defeat, and
whom no one
can conquer?

(*The Dhammapada*)

A nineteenth-
century Tibetan
mandala of the 42
Peaceful Buddhas
and Bodhisattvas
(*opposite*).

the judgment

A nineteenth-century Tibetan mandala of the Wrathful Buddhas (*opposite*): 'They are but the benevolent Buddhas and Bodhisattvas, changed in their outward aspect. In you alone are the five wisdoms, the source of the benign spirits! In you alone are the five poisons, the source of the angry spirits! It is from your own mind therefore that all this has sprung.'

the initiate is now invited to reflect on the Wrathful Buddhas and the judgment of the fourteenth day: 'You are now before Yama, King of the Dead. In vain will you try to lie, and to deny or conceal the evil deeds you have done. The Judge holds up before you the shining mirror of Karma, wherein all your deeds are reflected. But again you have to deal with dream images, which you yourself have made and which you project outside, without recognizing them as your own work. The mirror in which Yama seems to read your past is your own memory, and also his judgment is your own. It is you yourself who pronounce your own judgment, which in its turn determines your next rebirth.'

(The Tibetan Book of the Dead)

the lotus mandala
of shamvara

The mandala of Shamvara, or Paramasukha Chakrasamvara, shows the god with his female counterpart, Vajravarahi, immediately surrounded by four female Buddhas – Dakini, Lama, Khandarohi and Rupini – to make up the pentad of Buddhas. Between each figure is a cup made from a skull and full of blood, symbolizing an end to the disintegration of the world of nature and the human psyche and the recovery of primordial unity. The globular lotus of this mandala opens into eight petals, the first of three rings of eight elements.

Even the gods long to be like the Buddhas who are awake and watch, who find peace in contemplation and who, calm and steady, find joy in renunciation.

(*The Dhammapada*)

A three-dimensional Tibeto-Chinese mandala to invoke Shamvara (the Supreme Bliss Wheel Integration Buddha) in gilt-bronze, 17th century.

An eighteenth-century gilt-
brass offering mandala
from northern China.

mount meru – an offering mandala

*t*he inner surface of the Tantric mandala is first *divided by two main lines, the* brahmasutra, *from north to south, and from east to west. At the intersection of the two lines is Mount Meru, the* axis mundi *at the centre of the horizontal plane of the mandala and also the equivalent of the median canal in the human body. Three-dimensional mandalas were sometimes made in dough for the ritual of offering to Mount Meru; these were not so much aids to meditation as direct communication with the axial centre of the world, surrounded by the four continents of the Indian cosmology: crescent-shaped Purra Videha in the East; triangular Jambudvipa in the South; circular Apara Godaniya in the West, and the square Uttara Kuru in the North.*

FROM DARKNESS
TO LIGHT

the mandala is an external support for meditation; it helps provoke the feelings and visions by which man can arrive at a sense of unity within himself and with the universe outside. This impulse towards a sense of at-oneness with the whole of nature can be favourably guided by the arrangement in solid form of rays, flowers, circles, squares, and the representations of gods and goddesses. Thus, the original impulse to find a formal support for the deepest spiritual feelings may become in itself a means of leading the whole man towards the discovery of his secret reality and true illumination.

This nineteenth-century mandala makes a strong play of colour and form to draw the individual through meditation to a state of heightened consciousness.

Through meditation the adept must find himself at one
with the still point of the bindu; this wooden example
from Andrha Pradesh wonderfully exemplifies the feeling
of movement to and movement from the centre.

bindu

tantric belief finds the most concentrated point of the universe and the ultimate goal of the individual in the bindu. This is the centre of the circle, the irreducible point from which everything moves and towards which everything is directed; it is one of the two keys to the mandala — the other being the polarities. The bindu has neither beginning nor end, is neither positive nor negative: it is the embodiment of psychic and spiritual totality. It also suggests the waves of vibration from the centre; the more the form is in flux, the more it becomes whole.

Transcending the elements is the bindu. As a centre, the point controls everything which is projected from it; such a centre is called *mahabindu*, or Great Point, and signifies the starting-point in the unfolding of inner space, as well as the last point of its ultimate integration.

(*Giuseppe Tucci*)

In the light of his vision he has found his freedom: his thoughts are peace, his words are peace and his work is peace.

(*The Dhammapada*)

the mandala of aksobhya

the microcosmic structure of the mandala reflects the five components of the human personality: Matter, Sensation, Motion, Karma, and Cognizance. Each of these is associated with a colour: white, yellow, red, green and dark blue respectively, which in turn profoundly affect the reading of a mandala. The principle of five is constant throughout the mandala; in this example (opposite) Aksobhya ('The Brilliant One'), one of the five cosmic Buddhas, is seated in its centre, with the other four gods around him. Outside the circle are the Bodhisattvas.

In many Schools of Buddhism the correspondence between macrocosm and microcosm is expressed in other terms. The five Buddhas do not remain remote divine forms in distant heavens, but descend into us. I am the cosmos and the Buddhas are in myself. In me is the cosmic light, a mysterious presence, even if it be obscured by error. But these five Buddhas are nevertheless in me, they are the five constituents of the human personality.

(Giuseppe Tucci)

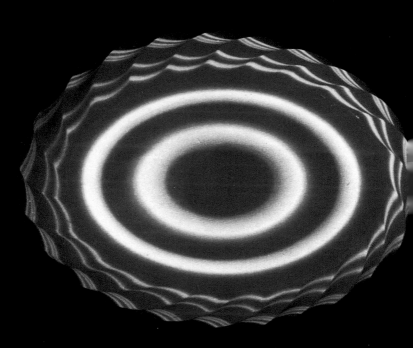

A stone from Rajasthan; the markings
resemble the orbital curves used to
represent the cosmos in certain forms
of mandala.

a natural mandala

the adept who discovers natural phenomena
incorporating the concentric rings of the classic
mandala may also use them as aids to
meditation and spiritual self-discovery. But the
ability to recognize the mandala innate in the
world outside and its symbolic significance is often
the result of a long and patient apprenticeship to
eradicate the ignorance which prevents us from
seeing the truth of ourselves and the cosmos.

Arise! Watch. Walk on the right path.
He who follows the right path has joy in
this world and in the world beyond.

(*The Dhammapada*)

serial meditation

the reading of the mandala is a progression, a
stage-by-stage process of illuminating those areas of the consciousness
which correspond to the parts of the world diagram. Step by step
the neophyte must move from the outer circle of his being to
successive interior states, aided by the movement from the perimeter
of the mandala to sectors closer to the central point. Yet the
experience yielded may differ from mandala to mandala, from yantra
to yantra, but the central point of complete catharsis cannot be
represented as being other than what it is. And so the adept may
meditate on a series of mandalas, realizing the various truths
expressed by the different patterns, but always moving
towards the spiritual fulfillment of the centre.

A Nepalese *tanka*
painted with nine
mandala-yantras,
to be meditated
on in series, *c.* 19th
century, ink and
colour on paper.

An eighteenth-century diagram from Kangru, Himachal
Pradesh, used for computing astronomical periods, but also
as an aid to meditation, ink and colour on paper.

the makeshift mandala

*t*he achievement of wholeness at the centre of an individual's
being can be aided by virtually any phenomenon or diagram
which provokes the appropriate forms of meditation. In Tantra
the creative process of worship may be focused by diagrammatic
forms initially intended for other purposes. These can be
permanent, for long-term use; others are ephemeral, perhaps in
sand or mud, to be destroyed after their immediate use as
meditational icons. There does persist a belief, however, that a
power diagram which is used over a long period does accrue
special significance and potency to itself.

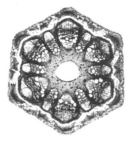

the yogi and his symbols

An eighteenth-century representation from Rajasthan of various systems and forms which can be used by the adept to comprehend the world and its structures; his whole body must be brought into harmonious accord with the elements, the *pancha-buta* of the cosmos: earth, fire, air, water and ether. In this diagram the neophyte has yet to embark upon his journey of self-liberation – a state symbolized by his bound hands.

the choice for the initiate of aids to lead him to a full comprehension of the cosmos is wide indeed, from mandala-yantras of varying complexity, pentacles, swastikas, and calligraphic diagrams. Once the neophyte has achieved catharsis, finding himself at one with whatever cosmic representation he is using, then he has access to total knowledge, even if only for a moment. Beyond and above the earthly plane is the Vajradhara, the Absolute, at which point the mandala may be transferred into the mystic's own body.

An eighteenth-century Nepalese yantra intended to aid the
adept in the journey towards man-cosmos unity.

man-cosmos unity

both Buddhism and Hinduism place great emphasis on the point of self-realization when the mandala or yantra of the external world leads to the mandala of the individual. The symbols of the original mandala are now arranged in a similar form within the body. Ideally, the new centre of the mandala should be the brahmarandhra, the 'cavity of Brahmā' at the top of the head, the termination of the median canal which runs along the spinal column. This columnar structure is the equivalent to the central mountain of the universe around which are arranged the various celestial planes, themselves the equivalents of the various centres of the human body (chakras).

Leave the past behind; leave the future behind; leave the present behind. Thou art then ready to go to the other shore. Never more shalt thou return to a life that ends in death.

(*The Dhammapada*)

the chakras

*a*ccording to the
Buddhist teachings we are
bodhi *and* dharmakāya,
'Buddha essence'; for the
Hindu adept we direct
ourselves towards Śiva, the
'Supreme Consciousness'.
The force which moves
through us – the principle
of awakening – is seen as
a luminous point
ascending through five

stages from the perineum to the brahmarandhra. This light is equivalent to the Light of the World, the everlasting origin of all things; it moves in the centre of the individual, just as the centre of the external mandala symbolizes the first principle of the cosmos.

Seventeenth-century ink and gouache scroll-paintings (*opposite* and *right*) of the meditative centres (*chakras*) from Rajasthan.

A late
nineteenth-
century
representation
from Rajasthan
of the *chakras*,
with the full
flowering of the
Kundalini
principle shown
above the head.

the subtle body

the fusion of the individual with the universal, the awakening of the whole body as a reflection of the world of time and space, is the object of kundalini-yoga. This meditative discipline concentrates on the awakening of the coiled Kundalini, the female energy which must be awoken to unite finally with Śiva, the Pure Consciousness of the whole cosmos. When Kundalini is awakened she progresses like a serpent up through the seven chakras, the centres of consciousness in the body which may function as inner mandala-yantras, until she reaches the seventh, Sahasràra chakra, the seat of the Absolute (Śiva-Śakti).

A man should control his words and mind and should not do any harm with his body. If these ways of action are pure he can make progress on the path of the wise.

(*The Dhammapada*)

the transcendent realm

As the Kundalini force ascends the seven chakras of the subtle body, the adept may meditate on each of the power centres, either in its own right or with the aid of an external mandala-yantra. The sixth chakra, seated between the eyebrows, is known as Ajña; its associated element is the mind itself, represented as a circle with two petals and an inverted triangle. Of especial importance is its seed mantra, which is the most powerful of all sounds, the primordial vibration OM.

Where all the subtle channels of the body meet, like spokes in the centre of a wheel, there he moves in the heart and transforms his one form unto many. Upon OM, Atman, your Self, place your meditation. Glory unto you in your far-away journey beyond darkness!

(*Mundaka Upanishad*)

In the iconography
of Tantric Buddhism
the *chakras* may be
represented as highly
visual mandalas in
their own right;
from the power
circles of the subtle
body stretches a
network of channel
and energy centres,
represented here in a
seventeenth-century
Nepalese image of
the adept in
transcendent state.

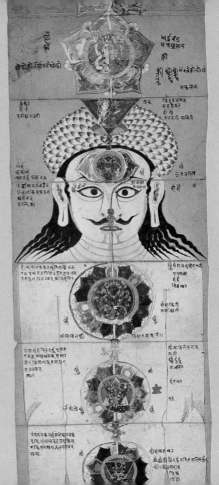

mantra

While *meditating on the mandala,
the postulant,* sādhaka, *will intone a
mantric sound, syllables based on sound
vibrations which parallel the stages of
understanding of the cosmos and the
awakening of the* chakras *of the subtle
body. The most potent of all mantras
is the sound OM, the representation
of universal knowledge. With two other
syllables, AH and HUM, associated
respectively with the throat and the
heart, it makes up the three Diamond
Seeds, which introduce the divine
essence into the body. This transfer is
realized by the placing of the hand
on the appropriate part of the body
as the syllable is intoned.*

**OM. This eternal
Word is all: what
was, what is and
what shall be, and
what beyond is in
eternity. All is OM.**

(*Mandukya Upanishad*)

'Monarch of all
sounded things': an
eighteenth-century
yantra from
Rajasthan expressing
the power of the
syllable OM.

THE WAY FORWARD

as a diagram of the cosmos, as a representation of our sense of wholeness and of at-oneness with the rest of the universe, the mandala has relevance and meaning way beyond the liturgies of Hinduism and Buddhism. People of widely differing cultures and historic periods have been drawn to the universality of its circular form, to its unique power to satisfy our longing for perfection.

When all desires that cling to the heart disappear, then a mortal becomes immortal, and even in this life attains Liberation.

(The Upanishads: The Supreme Teaching)

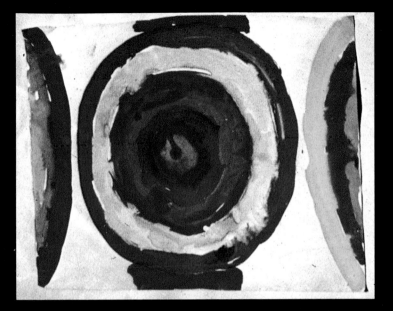

Experiments with groups of children
in the seven to twelve age group suggest that the
circular mandala form responds to deeply felt
visions of the universe. These images were created
after the children had sat in silent meditation for a
short time and had then been requested to paint
'whatever they saw'.

the golden flower

as a means of inner
healing and self-orientation,
the mandala form has
passed from East to
West. C.G. Jung noted
the form as one of the
archetypal symbols
issuing from the
collective unconscious;
as a representation of man's
need for wholeness, for perfection, it
could be used as a therapeutic device in the reintegration
of shattered personalities. Individual symbols and visions
could be accommodated within the form to concentrate
fruitful meditation, leading to a proper awareness
of self in relation to the world without.

Mandalas drawn
by a female patient
of C.G. Jung (*opposite*).

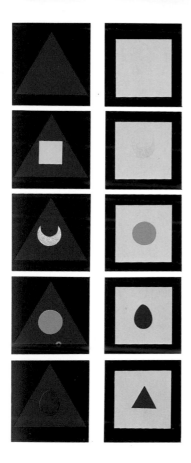

astral doorways

t*he fascination which the mandala and yantra forms held for Jung and his disciples was not the only example of the West adopting these Eastern forms. Symbols derived from these Tantric aids to meditation and the achievement of altered states of consciousness have long been valued by devotees of the occult. Tattva cards, a set of twenty-five coloured symbols, were used extensively by members of the Golden Dawn as aids to visionary experience.*

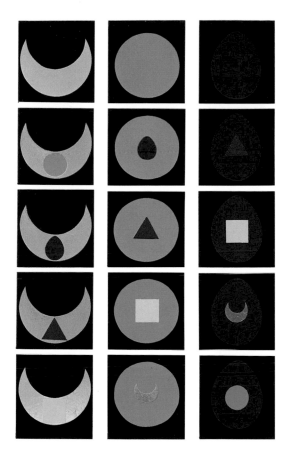

Modern Tattva cards, designed by Miranda Payne.

global mandala

the global nature of computer-based imaging makes the electronic recreation of the Śri Yantra mandala a peculiarly significant act: the symbolizing of self and the cosmos in a form which can be transmitted around the Earth. As the adept in meditation moves towards an understanding of all cosmic principles, so the electronic medium is revealing a world-wide communication system.

Therefore, in these nine triangles is expressed the process of divine expansion, which proceeds from the One to the Many, to Macrocosm and Microcosm and is the eclipse of non-Ego... This mandala, therefore, is considered as the exterior sacrifice in as much as it needs lines and letters in a visible pattern, but upon it is superposed, in a second phase, the interior sacrifice, the transposition of the mandala into the body of the initiate, identified mystically with Śiva, the Supreme Consciousness, which is mysteriously present within him.

(*Giuseppe Tucci*)

A Śri Yantra created in an electronic vibration field, from a film by Ronald Nameth.

Sources of Illustrations and Quotations

Prince of Wales Museum of Western Art, Bombay 22; Indian Museum, Calcutta 38; Gerd-Wolgang Essen 41–42; Robert Fludd, *Tomus Primus De Macrocosmi Historia*, 1617 21; Dr Joan Halifax 15; Maharaja Sawai Man Singh II Museum, Jaipur 37; Carl G. Jung, *Archetypes and the Collective Unconscious, Collected Works*, vol. 9, part 1, Routledge & Kegan Paul, 1959 74–75; Stanislaus Klossowski de Rola 66; Copyright British Museum, London 18, 35, 45; By courtesy of the Board of Trustees of the Victoria & Albert Museum, London 2; Ajit Mookerjee Collection 11–12, 27–32, 36, 39, 50, 54, 58, 60, 62, 64–65, 69, 71, 73; Ronald Nameth 79; Musée Guimet, Paris 46; Miranda Payne 76–77; Private Collection 1, 5, 7–8, 17, 23–24, 49, 56; Museum für Völkerkunde, Zürich 52. Sources of quotations: *The Theory and Practice of the Mandala*, London, 1961, © Giuseppe Tucci 13, 51, 53, 78; *The Upanishads*, Harmondsworth, 1965, trans. © Juan Mascaró 22, 68, 71, 72; *The Dhammapada*, Harmondsworth, 1973, trans. © Juan Mascaró 29, 40, 44, 51, 54, 61, 65; *Buddhist Scriptures*, Harmondsworth, 1959, trans. © Edward Conze 40, 42; *Speaking of Śiva*, Harmondsworth, 1973, trans. © A.K. Ramanujan 24.

© 1995 Thames and Hudson Ltd, London

British Library Cataloguing-in-Publication Data
A catalogue record for this book is available from the British Library

ISBN 0-500-06020-7

Printed and bound in Slovenia by Mladinska Knjiga